Housemates

LEVEL ONE   **400 HEADWORDS**

T0055623

OXFORD
UNIVERSITY PRESS

Great Clarendon Street, Oxford OX2 6DP

Oxford University Press is a department of the University of Oxford. It furthers the University's objective of excellence in research, scholarship, and education by publishing worldwide in

Oxford New York

Auckland Cape Town Dar es Salaam Hong Kong Karachi Kuala Lumpur Madrid Melbourne Mexico City Nairobi New Delhi Shanghai Taipei Toronto

With offices in

Argentina Austria Brazil Chile Czech Republic France Greece Guatemala Hungary Italy Japan Poland Portugal Singapore South Korea Switzerland Thailand Turkey Ukraine Vietnam

OXFORD and OXFORD ENGLISH are registered trade marks of Oxford University Press in the UK and in certain other countries

Printed in China

ACKNOWLEDGEMENTS

Illustrations by: Fred Van Deelan p 43

Commissioned photos by: David Jordan pp 1, 3, 4, 5, 9, 11, 12, 15, 17, 19, 21, 22, 26, 27, 28, 31, 32, 34, 36, 37, 39

The publisher would like to thank the following for permission to reproduce photographs: Alamy Images pp iv (Bondi Beach, Australia/Frank Chmura), 6 (Backpack/Mode Images Limited /Richard Gleed), 6 (Beer/archivberlin Fotoagentur GmbH), 7 (Surfing Board/Diomedia/Radivoje Davidovic), 18 (Status Quo/Pictorial Press Ltd), 18 (Log fire/Andrew Holt), 18 (Modern Kitchen/Elizabeth Whiting & Associates), 18 (Musical score/vario images GmbH & Co.KG/Bernhard Classen), 40 (house in Sydney/Sean Malyon), 40 (Suburb in Sydney Australia/David Hancock), 40 (Houses on cliff top, Sydney, Australia/J C Clamp), 42 (Sydney harbour bridge/David Cook), 42 (Sydney Opera House/K-PHOTOS), 42 (Darling Harbour, Sydney, Australia/Rob Rayworth); Corbis pp iv (Sydney Harbour and Harbour Bridge/Jose Fuste Raga), iv (Clownfish Over Luminescent Anemone/Stuart Westmorland), iv (Aboriginal Designs on Courtyard of Parliament Building, Canberra, Australia/Penny Tweedie), 6 (White Sand Beach, Venezuela/Sergio Pitamitz), 6 (Surfing in Oahu/Joe McBride), 6 (Mobile phone/Cooperphoto), 18 (Maggots/Eric Hosking), 30 (Breaching Killer Whale/Tom Brakefield), 50 (Sydney Harbour and Harbour Bridge/Jose Fuste Raga); Nature Picture Library pp12, 46 (Northern blue tongued skink/Robert Valentic); Photolibrary.com pp 24 (Assorted Foods on the Barbecue/Tom Eckerle), 39 (Wooden boomerang with aboriginal motifs); PunchStock pp iv (Uluru (Ayers Rock)/Goodshot), 18 (Man opening a window/Creatas); Rex Features p 6 (Pub crawl, Australia/Patrick Frilet); SuperStock p 18 (Rubbish/Pixtal); Travel-Ink pp iv, 50 (Sheep in Wagga Wagga, New South Wales, Australia/Trevor Creighton)

Cover: Getty Images (man holding mugs/Chris Windsor)

DOMINOES

Series Editors: Bill Bowler and Sue Parminter

Housemates

Alison Watts

Alison Watts grew up in Canberra, Australia, before moving to Sydney. She then spent several years working in Japan. She now enjoys the sunshine in Brisbane, Australia and – when she is not teaching English or writing – she is rock climbing, hiking, or socializing with friends. *Housemates* is her first book for Dominoes.

OXFORD
UNIVERSITY PRESS

BEFORE READING

1 Look at the photos of different places in Australia and match each one with a sentence.

a *Sydney*

b *Bondi Beach*

c *Wagga Wagga*

d *The Great Barrier Reef*

e *Canberra*

f *Ayers Rock*

1 ☐ It's the capital of Australia.
2 ☐ It's a country town about 500 kilometres from Sydney.
3 ☐ It's the biggest city in Australia.
4 ☐ People go there to surf in Sydney.
5 ☐ Its Aboriginal name is Uluru.
6 ☐ It's home to more than 1,500 different fish.

2 What do you know about Australia? Answer these questions.

a What language do Australians speak?
b How big is Australia?
c Which Australian animals do you know?
d What different things is Australia famous for?

Chapter 1
The Beach Sharehouse – 20/13 Old South Head Road

'I love playing with my dog, Jake,' I thought. 'But now I'm going to study at the **University** of Sydney and I'm going to live hours away from here, in the big city. How am I going to live without Jake?'

I was in my room in the country town of **Wagga Wagga**, with my **backpack** on the bed in front of me. I slowly put my last shirt into my backpack, and then I was ready to leave for the train station. Just then, there was a phone call. Mum answered it.

'Chris, it's **Aunty** Marj on the phone,' she called.

I didn't want to talk to Marj.

'Hello, Aunty,' I said when I got to the phone.

'Chrissy!' she cried.

I don't like the name 'Chrissy'. That's a girl's name. My name is 'Chris.'

'You're coming to Sydney, your mother says. You can come and live with me. I have two rooms, and I live near the university. What do you think?'

'Well, thanks, Aunty Marj, but I'm staying at a friend's house when I arrive,' I said quickly. It wasn't true. 'Can I call you next week?'

'Of course. I'm very excited about your visit.'

university people study here after they finish school

Wagga Wagga ˌwɒgə'wɒgə

backpack a bag that you wear on your back

aunty an informal word for your mother's (or father's) sister

I wasn't excited. I wanted to meet girls and go drinking in Sydney. I didn't want to visit my aunty.

At the train station my mum cried when I said goodbye.

'Bye, **mate**. Don't forget to go to **Bondi Beach**. The beautiful girls all go there,' my big brother Mike said.

I said goodbye to them and to my dog Jake. Then I got on the train. I was ready for my new life in Sydney.

◇◇◇

Sydney was big! There were a lot more people there than in Wagga Wagga. I took a taxi to Bondi Beach. What a beautiful place! There were a lot of nice girls on the beach, too. I wanted to live there. I soon found a **backpackers'** by the beach for the night.

The next morning, I began looking for my new home in Bondi. I bought a **newspaper** and looked at the **ads**, but the **flats** in Bondi were very expensive. I needed a **sharehouse**. I soon found an interesting ad. It said:

NEAR THE BEACH, 2 young **guys** with a sharehouse are looking for a third guy. $120 a week, call Josh on 9392 4979.

I rang the number at once.

'Hi mate,' I said. 'I saw your ad in the newspaper. I'm looking for a sharehouse. My name's Chris.'

'Hello. I'm Josh. Well, you can move in here with Adi and me at 20/13 Old South Head Road.'

So I went to meet Josh and Adi. Their flat was really nice. They had a big television in the front room, and they were nice guys, too.

'I'm going to study at the university,' I said. 'Are you students?'

mate friend

Bondi ˈbɒndaɪ

beach the land next to the sea

backpackers' informal word for a cheap little hotel

newspaper people read about things that happen every day in this

ad short for *advertisement*, you pay to put this in a newspaper

flat a number of rooms in a house where someone lives

sharehouse a flat where two or more people can live cheaply

guy man or person (informal)

2

'No, mate,' smiled Josh. 'We work . . . sometimes.'

'But not often,' laughed Adi. 'We like **surfing**, meeting girls, and drinking with our friends.'

Josh and Adi gave me the biggest room. From my window I could see the beach.

That night, Josh, Adi, and I went out to a **pub**. I met lots of their friends and drank lots of **beer**. At the pub Josh talked quietly with one of his friends, Rodney.

'Can you do some work for me later tonight?' asked Rodney.

'What are you two talking about?' I asked.

'Oh, nothing, mate,' said Josh.

surfing standing or lying on a flat board when the sea carries you back to the beach.

pub a building where people go to have a drink

beer a yellow or brown drink

We all had a good night, I think. Josh, Adi, and I left the pub and went back to the sharehouse very late. I went to bed at once, and I don't remember very much of the night because of all the beer.

The next morning I was in bed when I heard a noise at the front door. Someone **knocked** again and again, and two people called, 'Hello there! Open up!'

The noise didn't stop, so I went to the front door and opened it. It was the **police**!

'Are Joshua Warnick or Adrian Hughes here?' one of the police officers asked me.

'Yes, they are,' I said. 'Come in.'

Josh and Adi came out and spoke to the police. I went quickly back to my room. I sat next to my door and listened.

'Are you boys **stealing** things again?' one of the police officers asked.

'Of course not,' Josh answered.

'Stealing?' I thought. 'No, that can't be true. Josh and Adi are nice guys.' But then I thought again, 'Wait a minute. At the pub Rodney and Josh talked about doing some work later that night. Oh, no! Josh and Adi *aren't* nice guys. They're stealing things from people's houses.'

'We'd like to look through your flat,' one of the police officers said.

knock to hit strongly

police men and women who stop people doing bad things

steal (*past* **stole**) to take something without asking

'Do you have a **search warrant**?' Josh asked.

'Yes we do,' the police officer said. 'Wait here.'

The police went into Josh's and Adi's rooms. Then one of the officers came into my room. He looked under the bed, here and there, and went out again. I went after him into the front room.

'What's happening?' I asked.

The police stood with bags in their hands. In the bags there were expensive watches, **mobile phones**, and money. I looked at Josh and Adi.

'Sorry, mate,' said Josh. Then he spoke to the police.

'Chris is new in Sydney. He moved in with us yesterday,' he said. 'He knows nothing about all this.'

So the police took Josh and Adi away in the police car. And because I didn't have the money to live there **alone**, that was the end of the sharehouse in Old South Head Road. Where could I live now?

search warrant a paper that the police need before they can look for things in someone's house

mobile phone a phone that you can carry with you

alone with nobody

5

READING CHECK

Are these sentences true or false? Tick the boxes.

		True	False
a	Chris comes from a country town.	☑	☐
b	He's going to study at the university in Sydney.	☐	☐
c	He wants to live with his Aunty Marj.	☐	☐
d	He finds a flat in a newspaper.	☐	☐
e	He moves into a flat with two students.	☐	☐
f	Josh and Adi are nice to him.	☐	☐
g	They go out to a restaurant in the evening.	☐	☐
h	The next morning the police arrive at the flat.	☐	☐
i	The police take Josh and Adi away.	☐	☐
j	Chris lives in the flat after they leave.	☐	☐

WORD WORK

1 Unjumble the letters to write the words under the pictures.

a K C A P B C A K

.....backpack.....

b C H A B E

....

c G R U S N I F

....

d B U P

....

e R E B E

....

f E M I L O B   N E P O H

....

2 Find words from Chapter 1 in the surfboard.

universitynewspaperpoliceadflatknockstealalone

3 Use the words from Activity 2 to complete the sentences.

a Did you read the ...*newspaper*.... yesterday?

b Would you like to come for dinner at my .... tomorrow?

c Open the door! It's the ....!

d Did that boy .... some money from your bag?

e She's studying languages at Oxford ....

f Did you hear a .... on the door?

g I don't live with my family or friends. I live ....

h He saw an .... for an old car in a shop window.

GUESS WHAT

What happens in the next chapter? Tick two sentences.

a Chris goes to live with his aunt. ☐

b Chris sees Josh and Adi at the university. ☐

c Chris makes friends with an Italian student. ☐

d Chris finds a room in a big house with a rich man. ☐

e Chris finds a room in a house with a woman and her animals. ☐

f The woman has kangaroos and koalas in her house. ☐

Chapter 2
The Zoo Sharehouse – 6/18 Edward Street

I went back to the backpackers' that night.

The next morning I went to the 'uni'. That's short for university in Australian English. I felt very excited. I love learning new things and I wanted to learn about **Aboriginal** languages. There are lots of them. Mum and dad lived with the Aborigines in the Northern Territory before I was born. That's in the north of Australia and lots of Aborigines live there. Mum and dad told me lots of interesting stories about them when I was young.

On my first day of uni I met all the students and we talked. We didn't have **classes**. I met a nice guy, Fabio, from Italy. He spoke English well. 'I'm looking for a sharehouse,' I told him. We went to the uni **café** and looked at sharehouse ads there.

'Here's a **great** ad!' said Fabio.

It was for a house with a garden. Only one man lived there. 'I'm looking for a student to live with me,' said the ad.

I called at once.

'His name's Bruce, and I'm meeting him tonight,' I told Fabio.

After uni, I ate dinner at the backpackers'. Then I walked to Bruce's house. It was big and beautiful.

I knocked on the front door and waited. After some time Bruce opened the door. He was a 40-year-old man.

Aboriginal of black Australian people; Aborigines were the first people to live in Australia

class a time when students learn with a teacher

café a place where people go to drink coffee

great very good

'Come in,' he said. He looked very carefully at my shirt.

'Do you always wear old shirts?' he asked.

Before I could answer, he suddenly said, 'And where did you get those dirty shoes?'

Then he smiled and said, 'Would you like some **wine**?'

'Do you have coke or beer?' I asked.

He left the room, and I sat and waited. There were lots of **art** books and pictures in the room.

When Bruce came back, he had a bottle of wine in his hand. He gave me some, but I didn't drink it.

'What do you think of Picasso's work?' he asked.

'Who's he?' I asked.

'Don't you know?' he said. He looked angry.

'What work do you do?' I asked quickly. I wanted to talk about something different.

'I teach art at the University of Sydney.'

wine a red or white drink; when you drink a lot you feel happy and sleepy

art drawings and pictures

Suddenly he looked at his watch. 'Is that the time?' he said. He stood up and walked to the door.

'I'm sorry, Chris, but more people are coming to see my house tonight. Don't call me. I can call you,' he said. He opened the door and I walked out.

He didn't like me. Was it because I didn't know much about art? Or I didn't drink wine? Or perhaps he wanted a **housemate** with more expensive shoes and shirts.

That night Mum called me on my mobile phone.

'Hello Chris. Did you find a sharehouse?'

'No, I'm staying at the backpackers' tonight again. Can I call you tomorrow?'

I didn't want to tell Mum about Josh and Adi.

The next day I saw a new ad in the uni café.

Looking for a Sharehouse? Do you like animals?
Please call Cara on 9356 7782.

housemate
someone who lives with you in a sharehouse

Taronga
taˈrɒŋɡə

park a big garden that is open to everybody to visit

zoo a place where you can see animals from different countries

address the number and the street where somebody lives

I thought about my dog, Jake. 'Perhaps Cara has a dog,' I said. That afternoon I called her. After I left uni, I went to meet her at her house. There I met her dog, Toby. He was great! Cara knew a lot about animals because she worked at **Taronga Park Zoo**. Her house was nice, and my room was big. 'Well, do you want to move in?' she asked.

I moved my things from the backpackers' that night. I played with Toby for some time in the garden. After that, I felt tired so I went to bed.

The next day, I called mum. I told her my new **address**.

When we finished talking, I ate my breakfast.

Suddenly I felt something on my leg under the table. What was it? I looked under the table.

'What the—' I cried. There, on my leg, was a big **lizard**. I hate lizards! Cara ran into the room.

'What's the matter?' She asked.

I looked down at the lizard on my leg.

'What's that?' I cried.

'Oh it's only Bessy. She's a blue-**tongue** lizard.'

'Take it away!' I cried.

'Hey! Don't make all that noise! Bessy's afraid now, and all she wanted was to be your friend,' Cara said. She took the lizard in her hands and put it into a box. I ran into my room and closed the door behind me. Then I saw them!

There were two more lizards on my bed. I took my backpack and all my things, and I ran out of the house.

From the front door Cara called, 'Chris! Come back! Don't be afraid! They're only lizards!'

But I couldn't go back.

lizard a small green animal with a long tail

tongue the long soft thing in your mouth

11

ACTIVITIES

READING CHECK

1 Put these sentences in the correct order. Number them from 1–8.

a ☐ He meets an Italian student called Fabio.

b ☐ He runs away from the house.

c ☐ Chris spends his first day at university.

d ☐ He goes to see a man in a beautiful house.

e ☐ He finds one lizard under the breakfast table and two on his bed.

f ☐ Chris moves into a house with lots of animals.

g ☐ The man asks him about his old clothes.

2 What do they say?

1 I'm looking for a sharehouse.

2 What do you think of Picasso's work?

3 Did you find a sharehouse?

4 Well, do you want to move in?

5 Take it away!

6 Don't be afraid! They're only lizards!

a ☐ Chris's Mum asks him on the phone.

b ☐ Cara says to Chris when he leaves her house.

c ☐ Chris tells Cara when he sees the lizard in the kitchen.

d ☐ Chris tells Fabio at the university.

e ☐ Cara asks Chris when he visits her house in the afternoon.

f ☐ Bruce asks Chris at his house.

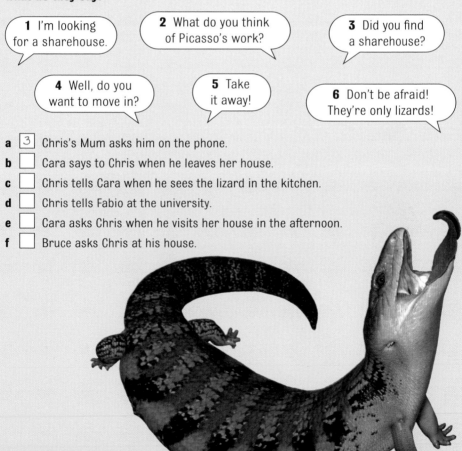

WORD WORK

Complete the word puzzle using the definitions.
Which Australian city is the secret word?

a this person lives with you in a sharehouse

b people need to know this to find your house

c a small green or brown animal with a long tail and short legs

d of the first Australians

e lots of animals from different countries live here

f it's in your mouth

g a big garden in a town for people to walk or sit in

h a red or white drink

i people go here to drink coffee

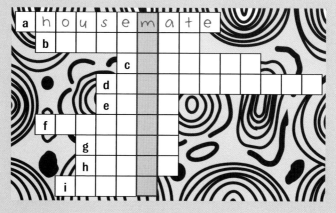

GUESS WHAT

What happens in the next chapter? Tick the boxes.

a Who does Chris move in with?
  1 ☐ His friend Fabio.
  2 ☐ Two of Fabio's friends.
  3 ☐ His aunt.

b What's the new sharehouse like?
  1 ☐ It's very dirty.
  2 ☐ It's beautiful.
  3 ☐ It's very small.

c Why can't Chris sleep at night?
  1 ☐ The house is next to the airport.
  2 ☐ He hasn't got a bed.
  3 ☐ His housemates make a lot of noise.

d How long does he stay there?
  1 ☐ For one day.
  2 ☐ Two or three weeks.
  3 ☐ All year.

Chapter 3
A Band of Dirty Housemates – 2/23 Beach Road

I went back to the backpackers' again.

The next morning, I met Fabio at the uni café.

I told him about Cara and the lizards. 'So now I need a new sharehouse,' I said.

Just then, two girls arrived and said hello.

'These are my friends Lisa and Karen,' said Fabio. 'The three of us play **music** in a **band**.'

'Fabio's the singer,' said Lisa.

'Do you want to be in our band?' asked Karen.

'We want someone to play the guitar,' Lisa said.

'Look, I love music, but I can't play the guitar. I'm sorry.'

'Chris is looking for a sharehouse.' Fabio said.

'Hey, our housemate Susan is going to Europe today,' said Karen. 'You can have her room.'

'OK,' I said, but then I thought of something.

'Wait a minute! Do you have any animals?' I asked.

'No, only us,' Lisa and Karen said, and they laughed.

'OK. But do you steal things?'

'No, we don't!' the two of them cried.

'Do you have any more questions?' asked Karen.

'One more, yes. Can I move in today?'

'After five o'clock this afternoon, OK?' said Karen.

music singing or playing instruments

band a number of people who play music

Lisa wrote their address on my hand, and they said goodbye.

'Thanks Fabio,' I said. 'You're a good friend.' Then we went into class.

When I arrived at the backpackers' I found three boxes from Mum there for me. I opened them quickly, but they were only things to eat. 'What does Mum think – there aren't any supermarkets in Sydney?' I couldn't carry the boxes and my backpack, so I called Fabio. 'Can you help me move my things?' I asked.

'Yes, of course,' said Fabio.

When we arrived, I looked carefully at Lisa and Karen's house. 'It's very dirty!' I said.

'Oh, don't worry about that,' said Fabio. 'That's Susan!'

Fabio and I put my backpack and boxes on the bed in Susan's old room. I was tired. It was only 6 o'clock in the evening, but I wanted to sleep. I said goodnight to Fabio, and went to bed.

After only a short time I heard a noise. 'Is someone knocking on the door?' I thought.

I went to the front door, and opened it. But there was no one there. Then I went into the front room. Karen, Lisa, and Fabio were there.

'Hello, Chris. We're playing music. Do you want to listen?'

'No thanks,' I said. 'I'm going to bed.'

I went to bed, but they didn't stop playing, and I could hear the music all night. In the end I went to sleep.

The next morning, I got up at six o'clock. Lisa was in the kitchen before me.

'Do you want some breakfast?' she asked.

'She gets up early,' I thought.

Then she said, 'Good night, Chris,' and went to bed.

Fabio didn't come to class that day. Perhaps he went to bed at six in the morning, too. After class I felt happy. 'I'm not going back to the backpackers',' I thought.

But when I arrived in my street, I could hear the girls' music. When I opened the front door, there was lots of smoke in the house. 'Oh, no! It's a **fire**!' I thought at first. But I was wrong. It was cigarette smoke, lots of it. I hate cigarettes! I opened all the windows, and went to my room.

I called Aunty Marj.

'Can I come for dinner this weekend?' I asked.

◇◇◇

fire this is red and hot, and it burns

rubbish things that you do not want any more

empty with nothing in

Every day when I came home there was cigarette smoke everywhere. In the kitchen there were lots of **rubbish** bags. And there were lots of **empty** wine bottles. Only I took them out. After a week of this, I was angry. I spoke to the girls.

'Lisa, Karen, you girls never do any **cleaning**!' I said angrily.

'Sorry, Chris. But we can change. From tomorrow we're going to clean every day,' Karen said.

'And can you play your music in the day, take the rubbish out, and stop smoking all the time?' I said.

'OK,' Lisa said.

The next evening I didn't hear any music when I arrived in the street. When I opened the front door, there wasn't any cigarette smoke. I opened the kitchen door. There were no rubbish bags in front of me. I smiled.

◇◆◇

The next week was good. But then the music began at night again, and I couldn't sleep. The cigarette smoke was bad again. And the house was dirty again, too.

One night I felt hungry. I went into the **kitchen**, but the cigarette smoke came in through the kitchen door. I closed it. And then I saw them! There behind the door were all the rubbish bags from that week.

'So Lisa and Karen didn't take the bags out. They put them behind the kitchen door!' I cried. The bags had lots of **maggots** all over them. 'I can't live with maggots!' I said, and I left that night.

clean to stop something being dirty

kitchen the room in the house where people make things to eat

maggot a little fat white animal with no legs that eats rubbish

READING CHECK

1 Correct the mistakes in the sentences.

a ~~Chris~~ *Fabio* plays in a band with Lisa and Karen.

b Karen and Lisa's housemate, Susan, is going to university.

c When Chris moves in, the house looks very nice.

d Chris goes to bed late on his first evening in the house.

e He gets up in the night because of the police.

f When Chris goes home from uni, the house smells of flowers.

g Karen and Lisa want to change, they tell Fabio.

h For some weeks the girls are quieter and cleaner.

i Chris finds all the old rubbish bags behind the bedroom door.

WORD WORK

1 Match the word halves in the smoke to label the pictures.

an ~~ba~~ bish cle chen fi gots
kit mag mu ~~nd~~ re rub sic

a *band*

b ....

c ....

d ....

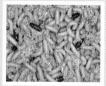

e ....

f ....

g ....

2 Complete Chris's email with words from Activity 1.

TO: mikepalmer@oz.com
FROM: chrispalmer@oz.com
SUBJECT: Hi!

Hi Mike!

It isn't easy to find a good sharehouse here in Sydney! I had a room in a house with two girls, but they were terrible! They're in a **a** ....*band*.... and they play **b** .... all night! They never **c** .... the house, they never take out the **d** .... , and the **e** .... is always dirty! The house always smells of smoke. One day I thought there was a **f** .... because of all the smoke!

Last night I found lots of rubbish bags behind the kitchen door – and there were **g** .... all over them! I moved out. But now I need to find a new sharehouse.

Chris

GUESS WHAT

What happens in the next chapter? Tick a box.

a ☐ Chris moves in with his Aunty Marj.

b ☐ Chris loves his new housemate very much.

c ☐ After some time Chris's new housemate doesn't want him in her house.

d ☐ Chris goes back home to Wagga Wagga.

Chapter 4

All Nice and Clean – 5/8 Birrell Street

After one more night at the backpackers' I found Shan Wen's ad at the supermarket. I always went there to shop, and she worked there. We usually said 'hello'. This time I asked lots of questions when I went to see the house.

'Do you have any pets?'

'No,' said Shan Wen.

'Do you take out the rubbish every night?'

'Oh yes. Of course,' she answered.

I didn't ask about stealing things. Shan Wen was nice, and her house was very clean. 'She doesn't steal,' I thought.

'Can you teach me some Chinese?' I asked.

I wanted to learn Chinese, because one day I wanted to visit China.

'OK,' said Shan Wen.

'Can I move in today?' I asked.

'I'm going to think about it. Can I call you this afternoon at three o'clock?' she said.

My mobile phone **rang** at one minute to three.

'Hello,' I said.

'Hi, Chris. It's Shan Wen here. You can move in now.'

I moved my things, and then went to the uni pub. My friends were there. I had lots of drinks, and then I got the **bus** to my new home.

There was no uni the next day. It was a weekend, so I slept late. When I got up, it was ten o'clock. I sat down and watched TV. I like watching different bands play

ring (*past* **rang**) to make a noise like a telephone

bus a big car that lots of people use to go from one place to another

20

on Saturday morning TV. But I couldn't hear anything because just then Shan Wen came into the room with the **vacuum cleaner**.

'How long are you going to be cleaning for?' I asked.

'Not long,' she said. After some time she finished. Now I could hear the music again. But then she began cleaning the TV, the chairs, and the table. This time I couldn't see the TV because she was in front of it!

'Why are you cleaning?' I asked.

'Because everything's dirty,' she said.

'I don't understand her,' I thought. 'The house is clean. There isn't any rubbish, and there aren't any maggots. What's wrong with her?' I went to my room and listened to the radio there.

Then my brother rang.

'Hi Mike, how are you?' I said.

'Good, mate. Listen, I'm coming to Sydney in two weeks. Can I stay with you?'

vacuum cleaner
people use this
to clean the floor
quickly

'Of course you can stay. You can meet my new housemate. We can have a **barbecue**.'

The next two weeks went very fast. I studied a lot, and I went to a pub most nights with my mates. I liked Sydney.

◇◇◇

I met my brother at the train station, and we walked through the city. He loved Sydney, too. When we arrived home, Shan Wen was there with the vacuum cleaner. After she finished cleaning, she went and had a **shower**. She had four or five showers every day.

We got the meat from the kitchen for the barbecue. Then Mike told me about life in Wagga Wagga.

After her shower, Shan Wen came to talk to us. But she left very quickly. She looked ill. I went after her.

barbecue when you cook meat on an open fire, often in a park or garden

shower water comes out of this. You stand under it to clean your body

'What's the matter?' I asked.

'I don't like meat. Please take it away!' she said.

'Sorry Mike, no barbecue tonight.' I said to my brother.

Mike and I went to the local pub for dinner.

The next day, I said goodbye to Mike and went to dinner with Aunty Marj.

She made me 'bangers and mash'. That's Australian for **sausages** and **potatoes**. I love it, and she knows that. We had a good dinner. 'Aunty Marj isn't bad,' I thought on the bus going home.

When I arrived, Shan Wen said, 'Can I talk to you?'

'She's angry about the meat,' I thought.

She handed me a paper and said, 'From tomorrow I want you to do these things in my house.'

I read the paper. It said:

Please clean your room every day.

Please don't bring meat, beer, wine, or your friends or family into the house.

Please don't watch TV when I'm cleaning.

Please don't wear shoes in the house.

Please don't come home after nine o'clock in the evening.

sausage pieces of meat in a long thin skin

'This isn't going to be easy,' I thought. But I didn't want to move back to the backpackers' again.

'OK, Shan Wen,' I said. 'I can do all this, I think.'

'Oh . . . but perhaps . . . it's going to be **difficult** for you. Perhaps you want to find a different sharehouse?' she said.

Then I understood. She didn't want me to stay.

'Am I the **problem** this time?' I thought.

I didn't have uni the next morning, so I went to an **Internet** Café. There I looked for a new sharehouse on the Internet.

potato (*plural* **potatoes**) a vegetable that is white with a brown skin

difficult not easy

problem something or someone that makes people feel bad

Internet you use a computer and a phone line to find different things on this

READING CHECK

Choose the right words to finish the sentences.

a Chris sees the ad for his new sharehouse . . .

  1 ☐ in a pub.

  2 ☐ at the uni.

  3 ☑ at a supermarket.

b On his first night in Shan Wen's house, Chris . . .

  1 ☐ stays out late drinking.

  2 ☐ stays in and watches TV.

  3 ☐ makes dinner.

c On Saturday morning, Chris watches TV and Shan Wen . . .

  1 ☐ goes shopping.

  2 ☐ watches TV with him.

  3 ☐ cleans the house.

d Chris's brother, Mike, phones and tells him . . .

  1 ☐ 'I'm coming to live in Sydney.'

  2 ☐ 'I'm visiting Sydney in two weeks.'

  3 ☐ 'I'm moving house.'

e Shan Wen looks ill . . .

  1 ☐ when she sees Chris's brother.

  2 ☐ when she sees meat – because she doesn't eat it.

  3 ☐ because Chris doesn't clean the house.

f When Mike leaves Sydney, . . .

  1 ☐ Chris goes to visit Aunty Marj.

  2 ☐ Chris goes to the pub for dinner.

  3 ☐ Chris says sorry to Shan Wen.

g Shan Wen can't easily tell Chris, 'Leave my house!' so she . . .

  1 ☐ gives him a very long list of things to do.

  2 ☐ begins eating meat with him.

  3 ☐ cleans the house again and again after him.

WORD WORK

Replace the orange words with the words in the sausages.

a The weather is beautiful. Let's have a dinner of meat in the garden tomorrow.

<u>barbecue</u>

ecrabube

b I usually go to school on the big long car for everybody.

_ _ _

sub

c This exercise looks not very easy .

_ _ _ _ _ _ _ _

ticufflid

d It's quick and easy to find things on computers talking on the phone.

_ _ _ _ _ _ _ _

treniten

e Have we got any big brown and white things?

_ _ _ _ _ _ _ _

eatostop

f We've got bad things with our new housemate.

_ _ _ _ _ _ _ _

brelpsom

g Wait a moment. My phone is making a noise.

_ _ _ _ _ _ _

grinnig

h The water for cleaning my body under isn't working in my room.

_ _ _ _ _ _

whoser

i That old thing for cleaning the floor makes a lot of noise.

_ _ _ _ _ _ _ _ _ _ _ _ _

mucavu creanel

GUESS WHAT

What happens in the next chapter? Tick the boxes.

	Yes	No
a Chris finds a sharehouse on the Internet.	☐	☐
b Chris moves in with one of Aunty Marj's young friends.	☐	☐
c Chris moves in with an older woman – a teacher at the university.	☐	☐
d Chris moves in with a beautiful university student.	☐	☐
e Chris finds a sharehouse with Fabio and Fabio's girlfriend.	☐	☐
f Chris loves his new housemate very much.	☐	☐

Chapter 5
Girlfriend and Boyfriend – 6/13 Fletcher Street

There were a lot of sharehouses in Bondi on the Internet. Could I find the right one for me?

Then I saw a sharehouse ad with a photo. 'She's beautiful,' I thought.

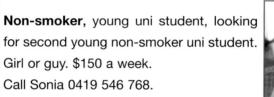

Non-smoker, young uni student, looking for second young non-smoker uni student. Girl or guy. $150 a week.
Call Sonia 0419 546 768.

We met that afternoon. Sonia asked me lots of questions, and we spoke for a long time. We talked about our uni classes and our interests. We didn't want to stop.

I moved in that afternoon.

'I think I'm going to live here for a long time,' I thought, and I put my bags on my new bed.

◇◆◇

The month went very quickly. Most days, after uni, I went home to study. But I didn't do much studying. I usually ate dinner with Sonia. After dinner we usually drank a bottle of wine, and we talked for a long time about everything. But soon I had **exams**.

'This week I must study a lot,' I told her.

'Me, too,' she said.

But that week wasn't any different. Most nights, after

non-smoker someone who doesn't smoke

exam a student takes these to see how much he or she knows

dinner and some wine, we wanted to talk. We didn't want to study. I liked Sonia a lot! 'Perhaps she likes me, too?' I thought.

Soon it was the last day of the first **semester**, June 28. It was Sonia's **birthday**, too. I finished my last exam. It was difficult, but I did OK, I think. I went to the shops to buy Sonia a video, **Life** *is Beautiful*. Then I went home to make her a birthday **cake**. When I heard her open the front door, I sang 'Happy Birthday'.

I gave her the cake, and she looked very happy.

After dinner and a bottle of wine, I said, 'Shall we watch this video?' I gave *Life is Beautiful* to her. She looked at it, but she didn't answer me.

'What's the matter?' I asked. 'Are you OK?'

'Thank you. But . . . I can't watch a video tonight. My . . . my . . . boyfriend's coming home.'

Just then there was a knock at the door.

I couldn't move. Sonia went and opened the door. A man walked in.

'Garth!'

'Sonia!'

semester the time between holidays at school or university; in Australia a semester is usually about four months

birthday the day when someone was born

life what you live

cake something that you eat on someone's birthday, after dinner, or with tea or coffee

They **kissed** and **hugged** for a long time.

I went to my room. I felt angry.

'Why didn't she tell me about her boyfriend?'

I couldn't sleep. I could hear them in Sonia's room. They talked and laughed very noisily.

The next morning I was very angry, but I didn't want to talk to Sonia in front of Garth.

kiss to touch lovingly with your mouth

hug to take lovingly in your arms

marine biologist someone who studies animals that live in the sea

whale a very big animal that lives in the sea and looks like a fish

'I'm going to buy a newspaper,' Garth said from Sonia's room.

Then I heard the front door open and close. I ran out of my room.

'Why didn't you tell me about him? How long is he staying?' I asked very quickly.

'I wanted to tell you but . . . he's a **marine biologist**. He studies **whales**. He's often away. He's going back up north to the Great Barrier Reef in two weeks.'

The next two days were bad. I talked to Garth, but he didn't answer. Sonia was very quiet, too.

I couldn't stay in the house with them.

It was the uni **holidays**, so I went home to Wagga Wagga. I had a great time.

◇◆◇

I played with Jake, and drank beer with my brother and my old friends. But I thought about Sonia a lot. Soon it was time to go back to Sydney.

'Is Garth going to be there?' I thought. I opened the front door. I couldn't hear anything. No, nobody was home.

I looked in Sonia's room. Garth's bags weren't there! I felt happy again. I made dinner for Sonia and waited.

When she arrived home, she was happy to see me. We talked, ate dinner, and laughed. Soon it was past twelve o'clock at night. We were tired.

'Let's go to bed,' she said.

'OK. Goodnight,' I said.

I went to my room. Then I stopped and thought. 'Does she want me to go to her room? No, she's got a boyfriend!'

I opened my door. Her door was open.

'Sonia,' I called, 'when is Garth coming back here?'

'In about four weeks, I think,' she answered.

'Oh no!' I thought. 'I love Sonia, but she loves Garth. Why is life always difficult for me?'

'Goodnight, Sonia,' I said, and I went back into my room and closed the door.

'I don't want to go back to the backpackers'!' I thought. And then I went to sleep.

holiday a time when you don't work or study

READING CHECK

Complete the gaps in the summary of this chapter.

Chris finds an ad for a sharehouse on the a) ~~Internet~~ . Sonia is a b) ....,
too and Chris likes her when they meet. Chris moves in and he is c) .... living
with Sonia. He goes to his classes and he doesn't often go out to the pub. In the evening
the two of them usually have d) .... , drink a bottle of e) .... and
talk a lot.

One evening, it's Sonia's f) .... Chris makes a cake for her and gives her a
video. But then Sonia's g) .... , Garth, comes home. Chris is really
h) .... and he goes i) .... for the holidays.

When Chris goes back to Sonia's house, Garth j) .... there. Sonia is very
k) .... to see Chris and the two of them have dinner. After dinner, they go
to bed.

WORD WORK

1 Circle nine more words from Chapter 5 in the word square.

K	C	N	E	J	Q	F	P	Y	L	A	R
P	F	O	R	A	R	G	U	J	K	B	A
I	A	N	S	B	H	C	B	P	D	I	E
F	L	S	I	E	B	L	I	F	E	O	N
S	E	M	E	S	T	E	R	O	S	L	E
A	X	O	Z	O	E	X	T	U	C	O	I
H	A	K	I	S	S	I	H	D	A	G	F
U	M	E	A	I	C	E	D	O	K	I	U
G	I	R	L	S	W	H	A	L	E	S	C
I	S	C	E	N	T	B	Y	A	O	T	G
H	O	L	I	D	A	Y	I	S	T	U	B
O	L	B	M	A	R	I	N	E	R	S	U

ACTIVITIES

2 Match the words from the word square on page 30 with the sentences.

a This person studies sea animals. marine biologist

b A time when you don't work or study. ....

c A year at university has two of these. ....

d Chris buys the video '........................ is beautiful' for Sonia.

e Chris makes this for Sonia. ....

f Garth and Sonia do these two things when he comes home.
.... and ....

g Sonia doesn't smoke. She's a ....

h This is the biggest animal in the sea. ....

i This is the day when you were born. ....

j Did you learn a lot? Teachers give this you to see. ....

GUESS WHAT

In the next chapter Chris goes to live with his Aunty Marj. What happens there? Tick four boxes.

a ☐ They talk about Marj's life when she was young.

b ☐ Chris likes Marj's house.

c ☐ Chris sleeps very well.

d ☐ Marj is angry when Chris comes home late.

e ☐ Marj makes good things for Chris to eat.

f ☐ Marj is happy for Chris's friends to visit him.

g ☐ Chris learns more about his parents when they were young.

h ☐ Sonia visits Chris at Marj's house.

Chapter 6

Home again —
2 / 63, Pitt Street

The next morning, I rang Aunty Marj.

'Can I stay at your house for two or three days?' I said.

'Of course you can, Chrissy. When are you coming?'

I wanted to leave Sonia's house quickly before I kissed her by accident. Of course, I didn't tell Marj that. I said, 'Can I come now?'

What could I say to Sonia? In the end I said, 'Goodbye, Sonia. I'm going to stay with my Aunty Marj.'

Sonia began crying, and she hugged me at the front door. 'Please stay,' she said. 'I love you.'

'What? What did you say?' I asked her quickly.

'Nothing. You must go. Your Aunty's waiting for you.'

The two of us cried then. I looked down, and walked

away. I didn't look back. I didn't want Sonia to see me crying.

I didn't want to go to Marj's with red eyes, so I went to a café on the beach. I sat and thought, 'Am I doing the right thing?' Then I had a coffee, and I felt better.

Aunty Marj was very happy to see me. She was in the front garden when

I arrived. I put my bags in my room, and we had a Coke. I didn't like Marj's house. It was an old woman's house. There were **dolls** everywhere. She **collected** clocks, too. They were in every room of the house. I didn't like that! We talked all afternoon. We looked at photos of my brother and me, from when we were children. She told me about her life when she was young.

'I was a **crazy hippy** then,' she said. 'Look at this.'

She gave me an old photo. She was in long **pants** with flowers on them. She was on the beach with friends, and she had something in her hand. It was a big cigarette, I think. This was a very different Aunty Marj for me!

Marj made me dinner, and to finish we ate some of her apple cake. It's famous in our family, and it was great.

I slept very well in my bed at Aunty Marj's house that night.

The next day after uni, I went to the uni pub with Fabio, and he talked about his holidays. 'I went on a surfing holiday for ten days and I had a great time,' he said. 'I met people from lots of different countries. I **fell in love with** Mika, a girl from Japan. She lives in Brisbane so I want to move there.' Then I told Fabio about Sonia and her boyfriend, Garth. Fabio said, 'You did the right thing!'

That night, I got home late. Aunty Marj was in bed. I was very quiet, but she heard me and came out of her room.

'Is she going to be angry?' I thought, but she wasn't.

She said, 'Hi Chrissy, your dinner's on the table.'

'I like staying here,' I thought.

'Marj,' I said.

'Yes, Chrissy?'

'Can my friends visit here sometimes?'

doll a small toy person that a child plays with

collect to have a number of things of one kind because you are interested in them

crazy thinking differently from most people

hippy people who lived in the 1960s, had long hair, and wore clothes with flowers on them

pants trousers

fall (*past* **fell**) **in love with** to begin to love someone

'Of course,' she said. 'But you must do the cleaning sometimes, too.'

'Can I drink beer?'

'Are you going to give me some, too? I love it!' she laughed.

'Perhaps living with Marj is the best thing to do?' I thought. 'Perhaps Aunty Marj is going to be the best housemate for me?'

She didn't steal, I knew that. She cleaned, but not all the time. And my friends could visit me when they wanted. We could drink beer, and eat meat here, too. There weren't any lizards. And Aunty Marj liked watching the **cricket** on TV, so I could watch it with her.

I couldn't forget about the dolls, the clocks, and her calling me 'Chrissy' all the time, but I could live with those small things.

'Can I stay here for a long time?' I asked.

cricket a sport that teams of eleven men play with a wooden bat and a hard red ball

'Of course,' she said. 'It can be difficult to find good housemates, I know.'

'Yes – very difficult! Did you live in a sharehouse when you were younger?' I asked.

'Of course!' she said. 'At first I lived with your mum. But then she fell in love with your dad and moved in with him.'

'Did you live with mum? What did you do?'

'I told you; we were crazy hippies. We were students at the time, but we didn't study much.' She gave me a photo to look at.

'And who did you live with after mum?' I asked.

'I moved into a big sharehouse with six people. But I only stayed there for three months because the building was very old. I couldn't have a shower or make dinner there,' she said.

'And what did you do when you left that house?' I asked.

'Then I fell in love with a young man.'

'Who? How did you meet him?' I asked quickly. So Aunty Marj liked men when she was younger! I didn't know that. She always said bad things about them.

'His name was Sam. He was from South Africa, and he was beautiful.'

'Were you housemates?' I asked.

'Yes. I moved in with Sam and his mate, Bec. But soon after I moved in, Bec moved out to Canberra. She went there to be a school teacher. She met a nice boy in Canberra, and they had lots of children.'

'And what happened with Sam? Did you live with him for a long time?'

'Well . . . we lived in Sydney for two years, but he **missed** his family. He wanted to go back home,' she said.

'So he left?'

miss to want something that you once had, but that you don't have now

35

'Yes. But I wanted to be with him, so I went with him to Durban in South Africa. I loved his family. His sister and father and I watched the cricket every day.'

'Did you like South Africa?' I asked.

'I loved it. But I missed Sydney. I couldn't get work in Durban, and it was very far from here, and very expensive to come back home for holidays.'

'Did you come back to Australia alone?' I asked.

'Yes, I did. Did I do the right thing? I don't know. Sam wanted me to stay, but . . .' she began, and then she stopped. She didn't look very happy.

'Do you speak with Sam these days?' I asked.

'No. But after twenty-five years I love him to this day,' she said, and she looked down.

I was quiet. What could I say?

In the end Marj spoke,'Oh, I forgot. These are for you.'

She gave me some flowers and a letter.

'They arrived this afternoon.'

'For me? Who are they from?'

'I don't know, Chrissy. Read the letter!'

I quickly went to my room and opened it.
I began reading.

> Hi Chris,
>
> I'm very sorry I didn't tell you about Garth. I rang
> him when you left. I told him everything. 'I love
> Chris and I want to be with him,' I said. Garth was
> very angry, and I feel bad about it. But it's true.
> I love you! Please call me!
>
> Love, Sonia XX

I came out of my room.

'Who's the letter from?' asked Aunty Marj.

'Oh, only one of my old housemates,' I said.

'Oh, I see.'

'Marj,' I said, 'Sam's important to you. You must write to
him in South Africa.'

'Perhaps you're right,' Aunty Marj said, and she smiled.

READING CHECK

Match the first and second parts of the sentences.

a Chris wants to leave Sonia's house

b He asks his aunt,

c There are lots of dolls and clocks

d His aunt tells him

e Fabio wants to move to Brisbane

f When Chris gets home late,

g When Aunty Marj was young,

h Aunty Marj's friend Sam

i Sonia writes to Chris

1 about her life when she was young.

2 and tells him, 'I love you!'

3 Aunty Marj leaves his dinner on the table for him.

4 because his girlfriend lives there.

5 before he kisses her.

6 'Can I stay at your house?'

7 in Aunty Marj's house.

8 lives in South Africa.

9 she lived in a house with Chris's Mum.

The Northern Territories

Great Barrier Reef

● Ayers Rock

● Brisbane

Wagga Wagga ●   ● Sydney
         ★ Canberra

● Melbourne

WORD WORK

Write the words and phrases from between the boomerangs in the sentences.

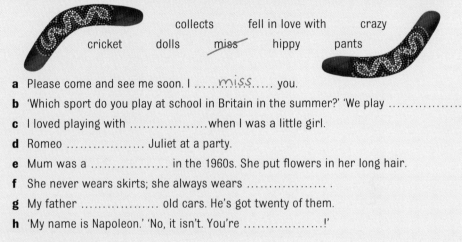

collects   fell in love with   crazy

cricket   dolls   miss   hippy   pants

a Please come and see me soon. I ......miss..... you.

b 'Which sport do you play at school in Britain in the summer?' 'We play .... '

c I loved playing with ....when I was a little girl.

d Romeo .... Juliet at a party.

e Mum was a .... in the 1960s. She put flowers in her long hair.

f She never wears skirts; she always wears ....

g My father .... old cars. He's got twenty of them.

h 'My name is Napoleon.' 'No, it isn't. You're ....!'

GUESS WHAT

What do you think happens to these people after the story ends? Use the phrases below to help you.

a . . . are boyfriend and girlfriend.   **d** . . . lives alone.

b . . . visits . . . .   **e** . . . writes to . . . .

c . . . steal things.   **f** . . . are on TV.

Fabio

Josh and Adi

Aunty Marj

Chris and Sonia

Lisa and Karen

Shan Wen

PROJECT A

1 Read the ads for three sharehouses and match them with the photos.

a

SHAREHOUSE with great views of the sea. Two uni students are looking for a non-smoker to share a new flat near the harbour. Girl or guy OK. No animals.

1

b

A ROOM with a family in a big house in the Sydney suburbs. Garden pool to share; your own bedroom and living room. Great for English language students.

2

c

SYDNEY CENTRE. Guy with old house in quiet city centre street is looking for someone to share with. No students. Small house, ten minutes walk from shops and harbour.

3

2 Which sharehouse would you like to live in? Why?

3 Amy is living in a new sharehouse. Read her letter. Which sharehouse is it?

Dear Eric,

I'm living in a sharehouse with two girls. They're uni students and I'm having a great time with them.

The flat is in a new building near the harbour. It's five minutes walk to the water and ten minutes to the shops and the university.

It's a big flat. There are three bedrooms and a big living room. My bedroom is the smallest, but I love it because you can see the harbour from the window. There's a garden but there isn't a pool.

I do the shopping and cleaning with my housemates. In the evening we have dinner and then we study. Two or three times a week we go running and at weekends the three of us go out to the cinema.

Please come and visit me soon!

Lots of love

Amy

4 Choose a different sharehouse ad. You are living there now. Write a letter about it to a friend.

PROJECT B

1 **Read about the tour of Sydney and complete the sentences on page 43.**

A Walking Tour of Sydney
by Jenny Betts

Sydney is one of the most beautiful modern cities in the world. It's got a beautiful harbour, interesting buildings and the weather is great. Do you have only one day in Sydney? Then you must visit our beautiful harbour.

Begin your morning with a visit to Sydney Harbour Bridge. You can walk across it, take a tour, or go up it.

Next, walk through the streets next to the bridge and look at the art galleries and shops there. Visit the Museum of Modern Art before you go to Circular Quay.

Walk along the harbour to Sydney Opera House. This is a great place to take photos. On Sundays you can buy things at a street market next to the water.

Then walk along the harbour to the beautiful Botanic Gardens. After that, walk along to Woolloomoolloo. There you can eat at Harry's Café. To finish your tour, and the day, walk into Kings Cross for night time entertainment and some great restaurants.

a The tour takes . . .

   1 ☐ two hours.   **2** ☐ a day.   **3** ☐ a week.

b You go on the tour . . .

   1 ☐ by bus.   **2** ☐ by boat.   **3** ☐ on foot.

c On the tour you see . . .

   1 ☐ the Opera House.   **2** ☐ Taronga Zoo.   **3** ☐ the University.

2 **Read about the tour again and mark the route on the map.**

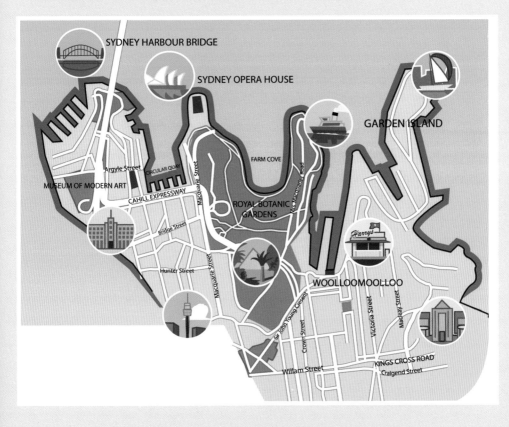

3 Think of a walking tour in your hometown. Make notes about the things to see and do on the tour in order.

	Place	What to see / do there
1		
2		
3		
4		
5		
6		
7		
8		

4 Write a description of your tour. Use words from the table to help you organize your description.

Talking about your town / city

What's good about it? ⟶ It's got . . .

What's the best thing to visit? ⟶ You must visit . . .

The tour

Where does it begin? ⟶ Begin with a visit to . . .

Where does it go next? ⟶ Next . . .
⟶ Walk through / along / to / into . . .
⟶ After that . . .

What can you do there? ⟶ This is a great place to . . .
⟶ There you can . . .

Where does it finish? ⟶ To finish your tour . . .

5 Draw a map of your tour and put some photos with it.

GRAMMAR CHECK

There is and there are: affirmative and negative

We use there is and there are to talk about the things and people in a place.
We use there is with singular nouns, and there are with plural nouns.

There's a backpack on the floor. (= There is)

There are lizards in Cara's house.

We often use there's as a short form of there is.
Negative forms are there isn't and there aren't.

There isn't a dog at Aunty Marj's house, and there aren't any lizards.

With there is/there are we can use some.
With there isn't/there aren't we can use any.

There is some wine at Bruce's house.

There isn't any beer.

1 Complete the sentences with *there is, there isn't, there are,* or *there aren't*.

a In the newspaper ...there are... some
   ads for sharehouses.

b In the front room of Josh and Adi's flat
   .... a big television.

c .... some watches and mobile
   phones in the bags.

d At Bruce's house .... a lot of art
   books.

e .... any beer at Bruce's house.

f .... any animals at Lisa and
   Karen's house.

g After Chris talks to the girls, ... any cigarette smoke in the house.

h .... lots of maggots all over the rubbish bags.

i .... a birthday cake for Sonia on the table.

j In Aunty Marj's house .... any young housemates.

k In her house .... clocks and dolls everywhere.

l .... a letter for Chris.

m .... some flowers for him too.

GRAMMAR CHECK

Imperatives

We use imperatives to tell people what to do or to give them advice.
We use the infinitive without *to* for affirmative imperatives.

Come and stay with me, Chris.

Negative imperatives start with do not or don't + infinitive without *to*.

Don't wear shoes in the house.

2 Complete the sentences with the imperatives in the box.

> call   ~~don't be~~   don't bring   don't call   don't make   don't open   don't play
>
> don't put   don't watch   open   put   stay   take   watch   write

a ...... *Don't be* ...... afraid. They're only lizards!

b .... the door at once. It's the police.

c .... all that noise!

d .... TV when I'm cleaning.

e .... the rubbish out, girls.

f .... me when you get this letter.

g .... the door. The cigarette smoke comes in.

h .... me Chrissy. My name is Chris.

i .... the cricket with me, Chrissy.

j .... the rubbish bags behind the door!

k .... to Sam, Aunty. It's important.

l .... meat into the house.

m .... away those lizards. I hate them!

n .... music at night. People want to sleep.

o .... with me, Chris. I love you.

GRAMMAR CHECK

Past Simple: affirmative and questions

With regular verbs we usually add –d/–ed to the infinitive without *to*.

Chris moved to Sydney. He wanted to find a sharehouse.

With regular verbs that end in consonant + –y we change y to i and add –ed.

study – Chris studied at the University of Sydney.

Some verbs are irregular. You must learn their past forms.

say – 'Come in,' he said.

In Past Simple questions most verbs take did + subject + infinitive without *to*.

Where did Josh and Adi live? Near the beach.

The verbs be and can are different. With them, we put the subject after the past verb to make past questions.

Could Chris live with Bruce?

3 **Complete the page from Chris's diary with the verbs in the Past Simple form, in the affirmative or in questions. Use the words in brackets.**

What a day that a) ...was... (be)! Yesterday I b) ....
(say) goodbye to Sonia and c) .... (leave) the house.
She d) .... (look) sad. I went to a café and
e) .... (think), f) '................. (I / do)
the right thing?' I g) .... (feel) better when I
h) .... (get) to Aunty Marj's. I like staying here. Then today I
i) .... (see) Fabio. 'Where j)................. (you / go) on your holidays?'
I k) ....(ask) him. He l) .... (tell) me about surfing and his
girlfriend, Mika. Tonight Aunty Marj m) ....(talk) to me about living in
Sydney when she n) .... (be) younger. 'I o)................. (have) a
boyfriend called Sam,' she p) .... (say). Then she q) ....
(remember) the letter and the flowers. 'These r) .... (come) for you this
afternoon,' she s) .... (say). I t) .... (read) the letter. It
u) .... (be) from Sonia. She loves me!

GRAMMAR CHECK

Making suggestions with shall we and let's

These are both used to make suggestions. After shall we and let's, we use the infinitive without *to*.

Shall we go to the pub?

Let's have some cake.

We can use let's not for a negative suggestion.

Let's not have any wine. I must study tonight.

4 Match each sentence with the right suggestion. Write the correct number in the box.

a 'I've got a wonderful video here.' [4]

b 'I need to find a room in a sharehouse.' ☐

c 'We can't have a barbecue at Shan Wen's house.' ☐

d 'Chris is right. The house is very dirty.' ☐

e 'I'm tired. It's after twelve o'clock.' ☐

f 'Dinner was very good, Aunty Marj!' ☐

g 'I want to see you soon, Chris!' ☐

h 'It's a nice day, and the beach isn't far away.' ☐

i 'I want to see you again, Sam.' ☐

j 'It's late, and everybody's in bed.' ☐

1 'Shall we go to bed?'

2 'Let's not play any music now.'

3 'Let's meet in Sydney, Marj!'

4 ~~'Let's not watch it tonight. My boyfriend's coming back.'~~

5 'Shall we have some apple cake now?'

6 'Let's clean it every day.'

7 'Shall we go to the pub for dinner then?'

8 'Let's go surfing!'

9 'Let's go to the uni café and look at the ads.'

10 'Let's meet tonight, Sonia!'

GRAMMAR

Time clauses with before, after, and when

In time clauses, we can use before, after, and when to link actions. When we write the time clause first, we must use a comma.

before links a later action with an earlier action.

Before Chris went to Sydney, his Aunty Marj called him.

Aunty Marj called Chris before he went to Sydney.

after links an earlier action with a later action.

After Chris left uni, he went to meet Cara.

Chris went to meet Cara after he left uni.

when links two actions close in time, where the first action is the reason for the second action.

When Chris saw lizards on his bed, he ran out of the house.

Chris ran out of the house when he saw lizards on his bed.

5 **Complete the sentences with *before*, *after*, or *when*.**

a ..After.. the police took Josh and Adi away, Chris left Old South Head Road.

b .... Chris went to Lisa and Karen's flat, he got three boxes from his mother.

c .... Chris went into the kitchen, he found rubbish bags behind the door.

d Chris asked Shan Wen a lot of questions .... he moved into her house.

e Lisa went to bed .... she met Chris in the kitchen.

f .... Chris met Sonia, they talked for a long time.

g .... Chris took his bags to his aunty's, he went to a café on the beach.

h Chris sang 'Happy birthday' .... he heard Sonia open the front door.

i .... Chris said goodbye to Mike, he went to dinner with Aunty Marj.

j Aunty Marj moved into a sharehouse .... Chris's mum moved in with his dad.

k .... the police looked in Josh and Adi's rooms, they found watches, phones, and money.

GRAMMAR CHECK

Countable and uncountable nouns: much, many, a lot of, and lots of

We use much with uncountable nouns, and we use many with countable nouns.
We usually use much and many in questions and negatives.

How much meat have we got, Mike? There isn't much meat.

How many cheap sharehouses are there in Bondi? There aren't many cheap sharehouses in Bondi.

In other sentences we usually use a lot of or lots of. There is not much difference between lots of and a lot of. We can use them both with countable and uncountable nouns.

Chris drank lots of/a lot of beer at the pub with Josh and Adi.

Cara has lots of/a lot of animals in her house.

6 Complete the sentences with *much, many, a lot of* or *lots of.*

a There are .a.lot.of. people in Sydney – more than in my town of Wagga Wagga.

b How .... beer did we drink last night?

c How .... different Aboriginal languages are there?

d Bruce's house was big, but not .... people lived there.

e There were .... animals at Cara's house.

f There wasn't .... wine in Karen and Lisa's house.

g But there were .... empty bottles!

h Chris could see .... cigarette smoke in the house.

i Has Chris got .... questions to ask Shan Wen about her house?

j Shan Wen liked to be clean, so she had .... showers every day.

k Chris didn't do .... work at Sonia's house, because he wanted to talk to her all the time.

l How .... clocks are there in Aunty Marj's house?

GRAMMAR CHECK

Gerund as object

The gerund (–ing form) is the noun form of the verb. We can use it as object after certain verbs and expressions.

Chris hates smoking.

Cara likes working with animals.

With most gerunds we add –ing to the verb.

talk – talking

When the verb ends in consonant + –e, we remove the e and add –ing.

live – living   *write – writing*

When the verb has one syllable and ends with one vowel and one consonant, we double the consonant before adding –ing.

put – putting   *stop – stopping*

7 Complete the sentences with the *–ing* form of the verbs in the box.

~~clean~~	collect	eat	knock	listen to	live
make	open	speak	put	steal	surf

a When Chris watched TV, Shan Wen began ..cleaning.. the room.

b Josh and Adi liked .... things from people's houses.

c Chris stopped .... at Beach Road because the house was very dirty.

d At Bondi Beach lots of people go ....

e After Chris talked to them, Karen and Lisa began .... the rubbish behind the kitchen door.

f When Aunty Marj came back to Sydney, she finished .... with Sam.

g Aunty Marj loved .... dolls and clocks.

h Mike and Chris stopped .... a barbecue and went to the pub.

i When Chris saw all the smoke, he began .... the windows.

j When Chris opened the door, the police stopped ....

k Fabio liked .... music with Karen and Lisa.

l Chris loved .... Aunty Marj's apple cake.

DOMINOES THE STRUCTURED APPROACH TO READING IN ENGLISH

Dominoes is an enjoyable series of illustrated classic and modern stories in four carefully graded language stages – from Starter to Three – which take learners from beginner to intermediate level.

Each *Domino* reader includes:

- **a good story** to read and enjoy
- **integrated activities** to develop reading skills and increase active vocabulary
- **personalized projects** to make the language and story themes more meaningful
- **seven pages of grammar activities** for consolidation.

Each *Domino* pack contains a reader, plus a MultiROM with:

- **a complete audio recording of the story,** fully dramatized to bring it to life
- **interactive activities** to offer further practice in reading and language skills and to consolidate learning.

If you liked this Level One *Domino*, why not read these?

Studio Five
Anthony Manning

Fay loves making The Friends' Hour for Studio Five, but her boss – Jason – is always angry with her. One day, a young man – Simon Jones – phones her show. Soon Fay must find Simon, and work hard to keep her job. Then her best friend – Wing –stops helping her. What can Fay do now? Can she and Wing stay friends?

Book ISBN: 978 0 19 424765 8
MultiROM Pack ISBN: 978 0 19 424729 0

Twenty Thousand Leagues Under the Sea
Jules Verne

When ship after ship goes down in the Atlantic, Dr Pierre Aronnax and his servant, Conseil, journey from Paris to learn more. What – or who – is attacking these ships?

Aronnax, Conseil, and the Canadian, Ned Land, find the answer to this question when they meet the strange Captain Nemo.

After a long journey under the sea in Nemo's submarine, the Nautilus, the doctor and his friends plan to leave for the surface.

But how can they escape?

Book ISBN: 978 0 19 424771 9
MultiROM Pack ISBN: 978 0 19 424735 1

You can find details and a full list of books in the *Dominoes* catalogue and Oxford English Language Teaching Catalogue, and on the website: www.oup.com/elt

Teachers: see www.oup.com/elt for a full range of online support, or consult your local office.

	CEF	Cambridge Exams	IELTS	TOEFL iBT	TOEIC
Starter	A1	YLE Movers	–	–	–
Level 1	A1–A2	YLE Flyers/KET	3.0	–	–
Level 2	A2–B1	KET-PET	3.0-4.0	–	–
Level 3	B1	PET	4.0	57-86	550